Memories of Survival
A gift from
CYPRESS
2014

Memories of Survival

OCTOBER 31 1942, AFTER OUR NIGHT IN THE FIELDS, MANIA AND I WENT BACK TO KSIEZOMIESZ TO DUDZINSKA'S HOUSE, WHERE MANIA HAD WORKED. WHEN SHE SAW US, SHE PUSHED US OUT INTO THE FIELDS AND SAID, "GOD HELP YOU, RUN FOR YOUR LIVES! EVERYONE KNOWS YOU ARE HERSH'S DAUGHTERS, AND THE GESTAPO WERE JUST HERE."
ESTHER NISENTHAL KRINITZ 1994

ESTHER NISENTHAL KRINITZ
AND BERNICE STEINHARDT

ART AND REMEMBRANCE
WASHINGTON, DC

Childhood Home pages 6/7: embroidery on linen, 1977. 55" W x 48" H.   *The Tucin River* page 8: embroidery on linen, 1978. 56" W x 48" H.   *Ruven* page 9: embroidery and fabric collage, with fabric wash, 1996. 26" W x 31" H.   *Shavuot* page 10: embroidery and fabric collage, 1994. 20" W x 23" H.   *Rosh Hashonah* page 12: embroidery and fabric collage, 1996. 32" W x 42" H.   *Passover* pages 14/15: embroidery and fabric collage, 1998. 32" W x 20" H.   *Nazis arrive in Mniszek* pages 16/17: embroidery and fabric collage, 1993. 54" W x 41" H.   *Digging Trenches* page 18: embroidery and fabric collage, 1996. 23" W x 31" H.   *Toothache* page 20: embroidery and fabric collage, 1997. 29" W x 33" H.   *Goscieradow* pages 22/23: embroidery and fabric collage, 1994. 33" W x 29" H.   *Erev Pesach* page 25: embroidery and fabric collage, 1993. 38" W x 43" H.   *Janiszow (Heaven and Hell)* pages 26/27: embroidery and fabric collage, 1994. 40" W x 30" H.   *The Pine Forest* page 28: embroidery and fabric collage, 1996. 28" W x 34" H.   *Dawn Raid* page 30: embroidery and fabric collage, 1992. 36" W x 38" H.   *Dawn Raid 11* page 31: embroidery and fabric collage, 1992. 24" W x 22" H.   *Fleeing Across the Fields* page 32: embroidery on cloth, 1992. 22" W x 22" H.   *Saying Good-bye* page 34: embroidery and fabric collage, 1993. 32" W x 39" H.   *Leaving for Good* page 35: embroidery and fabric collage, with fabric wash, 1998. 44 1/2" W x 44 1/2" H.   *The Jews of Rachow* page 36: embroidery and fabric collage, 1991. 42" W x 42" H.   *Dina* page 38: embroidery and fabric collage, 1994. 28" W x 32" H.   *Stefan's house* pages 40/41: embroidery and fabric collage, 1993. 56" W x 40" H.   *Ksiezomierz* pages 42/43: embroidery and fabric collage, 1993. 41" W x 24" H.   *Depths of the Forest* page 44: embroidery and fabric collage, 1994. 20" W x 20" H.   *Zebina* page 46: embroidery and fabric collage, 1994. 36" W x 44" H.   *The Sky is Falling* page 48: embroidery and fabric collage, 1988. 36" W x 37" H.   *The Well* page 50: embroidery and fabric collage, with fabric wash, 1994. 37" W x 37" H.   *The Bees* page 52: embroidery and fabric collage, 1996. 32" W x 34" H.   *Zayde* page 54: embroidery and fabric collage, 1989. 41" W x 38" H.   *Freedom* page 56: embroidery and fabric collage, with fabric wash, 1995. 32" W x 33" H.   *Maidanek* page 58: embroidery and fabric collage, with fabric wash, 1995. 37" W x 53" H.   *To Germany* pages 60/61: embroidery and fabric collage, 1998. 36" W x 31" H.   *Coming to America* page 62: embroidery and fabric collage, with fabric wash, 1996. 24" W x 24" H.

A NOTE ON THE ART

Esther employed a variety of needlework techniques in these pictures, including various styles of embroidery and fabric collage. Although she used a sewing machine for some of the stitching, most was done by hand. Nearly all of the pictures contain a hand-stitched narrative caption. For the early pictures that do not have stitched captions—the first two pictures of her home and the two dreams—she later came up with descriptive captions that we've used here. Sometimes the spelling of Polish place names differs in the stitched narrative and my commentary, where I've used the conventional spelling.

In addition to the pictures included here, Esther created two family portraits that, together with the others, make up the thirty-six pictures in the entire collection. One is a portrait of my father, Max, that Esther created after his death in 1998. The other is of my daughter Rachel as a two-year-old. Readers may find these images at www.artandremembrance.org, along with additional information on Esther's work.

—Bernice Steinhardt

Copyright © 2005 by Bernice Steinhardt and Helene McQuade   All rights reserved.

Designed by Christine Kettner   Second Edition   3 5 7 9 10 8 6 4 2   Printed in Singapore

Library of Congress Number 2010902793   Reinforced binding   ISBN 978-0-615-35727-0

TWP   2013

Visit www.artandremembrance.org

Contents

Childhood Home / 6

The Tucin River / 8

Ruven / 9

Shavuot / 10

Rosh Hashonah / 12

Passover / 14

Nazis Arrive in Mniszek / 16

Digging Trenches / 18

Toothache / 20

Goscieradow / 22

Erev Pesach / 24

Janiszow (Heaven and Hell) / 26

The Pine Forest / 28

Dawn Raid / 30

Dawn Raid II / 31

Fleeing Across the Fields / 32

Saying Good-bye / 34

Leaving for Good / 35

The Jews of Rachow / 36

Dina / 38

Stefan's House / 40

Ksiezomierz / 42

Depths of the Forest / 44

Zebina / 46

The Sky Is Falling / 48

The Well / 50

The Bees / 52

Zayde / 54

Freedom / 56

Maidanek / 58

To Germany / 60

Coming to America / 62

Introduction

My MOTHER, ESTHER NISENTHAL KRINITZ, was always different from other mothers. She was more beautiful, to be sure, with her petite figure, lovely face, and keen sense of style. She also sounded unlike other mothers, pronouncing *w* like *v*, *th* like *d*, and mixing Yiddish into her English.

But what set my mother apart most of all was the life she had led. Growing up in the middle of the twentieth century, in the biggest city of them all—New York—I lived in a world of TV, cars, skyscrapers, and subways. My mother, on the other hand, grew up in a little village of no more than a dozen families in central Poland, where people eked out small livings and raised their own food. This was not simply rural life, but rural life in another century, before cars and machines, where all labor was done by hand or animal.

My mother also saw things that no one else I knew had seen. When she was twelve years old, in 1939, she saw Nazi soldiers arrive in her village, drag her grandfather from his doorstep, and cut off his beard. She saw her cousins imprisoned in Nazi labor camps, from which they never returned. And when she was fifteen years old, she saw her mother and father and brother and sisters for the last time, watching them head to their probable deaths, as she struggled to survive.

All my life, I heard her stories—all of them. The stories of her mother's delicious cooking, the heavenly challahs and sponge cakes and matzos for the holidays. Of how sickly she was as a child, sneaking into the kitchen late at night to relieve the pain of the boils in her fingertips by dipping them into her mother's yeast-starter dough. Of how she nearly drowned in the river in her eagerness to follow her big brother, and never fully recovered her hearing in her left ear. Of the beautiful costume she sewed for herself for the May Day celebration when she was eight, with its brilliant red and green ribbons and lace trim. Of the trips she and her mother would make into the oak forests where the best mushrooms grew. Of the geese she raised and how she loved all the little goslings.

And then, of course, there were the stories of how she survived on her own. Of how she made up identities for herself and her sister Mania so that they could go to another village, someplace where no one knew them, and find work with people who were willing to accept them as Polish Catholic girls who had been separated from their family. Of how she would hide in the attic of the barn during Nazi raids. Of how she joined the Polish army, once the Germans had retreated from her village as the war drew to a close, and was part of the first army to reach Berlin.

I can't remember a time in my life when I didn't know these stories. Sitting at the kitchen table,

I would listen, transfixed, as my mother made our lunch or cooked our dinner, or did her weekly baking, rolling out the strudel dough or the dough for cinnamon rolls. These stories fed us, too.

As a child, I knew a girl whose parents had been in a concentration camp. I saw the tattooed numbers on their arms once, and asked her what had happened to her parents. She didn't know. They never talked to her about their experiences. My mother explained it to me like this: "Some people were broken by the war."

Still—how could they not tell? My mother couldn't keep from telling. It seemed to be the only way she could make sense of the extreme horror that had consumed her family and left only her and her sister.

She told us her stories, but she also wanted to write them down for us. In little notebooks, she wrote in Yiddish and English. But her English wasn't very good, and she wasn't really confident about her writing. She always told me that I would write her story for her, and when I was ten, I actually tried. I didn't get very far, though, before I realized that only my mother could tell her story. I told her so.

And so, years later, she went back to it. Over the years, she continued to write intermittently in a set of notebooks, filling up pages with stories that told of her courage and longing.

Her stories served so many purposes. They helped her to explain herself to herself, allowing her to examine in retrospect actions that she had taken instinctively on the spot. They helped her to relieve the intense pressure of memories by putting them into words, saying out loud what was running through her mind. Most important, her stories kept her connected to the people she had loved, kept alive her love for the family she had lost, and as well, their love for her.

In 1977, when Esther was fifty, she decided that she wanted her daughters to see what her childhood had been like, by creating a picture of it. She had no artistic training, but she was extremely skilled in sewing and embroidery, which she had started doing as a little girl. She knew she could stitch the picture she wanted to create, but she wasn't confident that she could draw it, so she asked my sister, Helene, to draw for her the picture she wanted to make: of her house, the neighbors' house, and her family. "But, Mom," Helene said, "I don't know what your house looked like! You'll have to do this yourself!"

Once again, on her own, my mother created the first of what eventually became a series of thirty-six embroidered pictures, illustrating the stories of her childhood and survival during the war. She used the skills she had—her powerful memory and eye, and her remarkable sewing technique—to tell her own story, in her own way.

Esther died in March 2001, at the age of seventy-four. She wasn't finished telling her story when she died.

But, finished or not, this is the story she left to share with us—all of us.

—Bernice Steinhardt

Childhood Home

"My childhood home in the village of Mniszek, near the city of Rachow (today Annapol), Poland. I am carrying water up the hill to our house; my sister Mania waits for me. My brother, Ruven, is standing with the wagon. My father and my sister Chana are in front of the house, along with my mother, who holds my youngest sister, Leah."

—Esther

MY MOTHER, ESTHER KRINITZ, grew up in a little village called Mniszek in central Poland. A dozen or so families lived in Mniszek, most of them Jewish, and many of them were related in one way or another to Esther's family.

This is how Esther's home appeared in 1937, when Esther was ten. The house, on a small hill, was built of split logs. The roof was thatched and the floor and walls were made of packed earth.

Everyone in the family worked. Esther's father, Hersh Nisenthal, was a horse trader. He had served in the Polish cavalry in World War I, and knew horses very well. Esther's mother, Rachel Prizant Nisenthal, raised chickens and geese, and sold the eggs and birds at the market.

Esther had one older brother, Ruven, and three younger sisters: Mania, who was two years younger; Chana; and Leah, the baby. As the boy, Ruven was expected to study and work for his father; the girls were expected to mind their younger siblings. It was also expected that Esther would become a dressmaker. When she was about nine, she started going to Juszia the dressmaker's house several times a week to learn how to sew.

The Tucin River

"Ruven and I swim in the river below our house, a tributary of the Vistula River. Mania and Leah tend the geese, while Chana stays at the river's edge. Farmers are coming back from the fields at noon."

—Esther

Ruven

"June 1937. After he came to my defense in a fight with my friend, my brother Ruven was afraid to come home, knowing that my mother, who had heard about the fight, had threatened to beat him. He spent the night in the horse barn. In the morning, after my mother left, I fixed him a bowl of borscht and crawled through the kitchen window to bring it to him. When I returned to my house after the war, and found a Polish family living there, I walked into the kitchen and stood in front of the window with my eyes closed, wanting to relive the feeling of that time when I sat close to my brother and watched him eat."

—Esther

JUNE 1937. AFTER HE CAME TO MY DEFENSE IN A FIGHT WITH MY FRIEND, MY BROTHER RUVEN WAS AFRAID TO COME HOME, KNOWING THAT MY MOTHER WHO HAD HEARD ABOUT THE FIGHT, HAD THREATENED TO BEAT HIM. HE SPENT THE NIGHT IN THE HORSE BARN. IN THE MORNING AFTER MY MOTHER LEFT, I FIXED HIM A BOWL OF BORSCHT AND CRAWLED THROUGH THE KITCHEN WINDOW TO BRING IT TO HIM. WHEN I RETURNED TO MY HOUSE AFTER THE WAR, AND FOUND A POLISH FAMILY LIVING THERE, I WALKED INTO THE KITCHEN AND STOOD IN FRONT OF THE WINDOW WITH MY EYES CLOSED, WANTING TO RELIVE THE FEELING OF THAT TIME WHEN I SAT CLOSE TO MY BROTHER AND WATCHED HIM EAT.
ESTHER NISENTHAL KRINITZ 1996

SHAVUOT 1938 MY BROTHER AND SISTERS FOLLOWED AS
I WALKED ON STILTS TO OUR GRANDPARENTS HOUSE.
                    ESTHER
        MANIA   RUBIN
        CHANA   LEAH

                    ESTHER NISENTHAL KRINITZ 1994

Shavuot

"Shavuot 1938. My brother and sisters followed as I walked on stilts to our grandparents' house."

—Esther

MY MOTHER LOVED THE JEWISH HOLIDAYS, especially the festival holidays. Her family went without most of the time, wearing patched and darned clothes, stretching meals with potatoes. In fact, for a while, Esther's mother, Rachel, earned some money by unraveling worn sweaters and reknitting them with the yarn.

But for the holidays, there were always new clothes, and—best of all— food! Somehow, Rachel always created feasts from the ingredients she had at hand: eggs, onions, potatoes, cabbages, chicken, and goose fat. And in summer: blueberries, strawberries, cherries, sour cream, cheese, wild mushrooms, cucumbers, and pumpernickel.

Shavuot is the harvest holiday, falling usually in June. In Mniszek, the first wheat would be growing, and Esther and her brother and sisters would cut through wheat fields to get to their grandparents' house. Esther was always something of a tomboy, and took pride in her physical feats. Her brother made her a pair of stilts, and she couldn't wait to try them out. Ruven was the one who made the toys, but Esther was the one to test them. She was so proud of the fact that she made it all the way to her grandparents' house without falling.

ROSH HASHONAH 1938. THIS WAS THE LAST ROSH HASHONAH SERVICE THAT MY ZAYDE, CHAIM, AND HIS NEIGHBOR, BARESH -- THE TWO PATRIARCHS OF THE VILLAGE --
CONDUCTED. SHABBOS AND HOLIDAY SERVICES WERE ALWAYS CONDUCTED IN SHMUEL'S HOUSE, ONE OF THE LARGEST AND NICEST IN MNIESZEK.
MOST OF THE FURNITURE WAS REMOVED, AND THE TORAH WAS PLACED IN A CLOSET DRAPED WITH CURTAINS.

ESTHER NISENTHAL KRINITZ 1996

ROSH HASHONAH

"Rosh Hashonah 1938. This was the last Rosh Hashonah service that my zayde, Chaim, and his neighbor, Baresh—the two patriarchs of the village—conducted. Shabbos and holiday services were always conducted in Shmuel's house, one of the largest and nicest in Mniszek. Most of the furniture was removed, and the Torah was placed in a closet draped with curtains."

—Esther

AS ONE OF THE VILLAGE ELDERS, Esther's grandfather Chaim—her *zayde*—used to lead prayer services for the Jewish families of Mniszek. Esther actually made the little red curtain in this picture, which is lifted to reveal the Torah behind it. Chaim is about to blow the *shofar*, the ram's horn used to herald the Jewish New Year, called Rosh Hashonah.

The room in which the services were held was only for the men; women and children were segregated from the men in a room next door. Esther would look through the doorway of this room, so proud to see her zayde leading the prayers.

My mother put a white border around this picture to distinguish it from the others. In the gold thread and braid that runs around the picture, she shows her reverence for Rosh Hashonah and Yom Kippur, the Day of Atonement—the holiest of Jewish holidays.

MARCH 1939. EVERY YEAR BEFORE PASSOVER, THE JEWISH WOMEN OF MNISZEK WOULD GATHER AT MOTTEL THE SHOEMA[...] MATZOS AND PASS THEM TO HIS SON YANKEL TO BAKE, EACH WOMAN WOULD MAKE THE DOUGH FOR HER OWN MATZOS, [...] MAKING THE DOUGH HERE, WAS ONE OF THE BEST DOUGH MAKERS BECAUSE SHE MIXED HER INGREDIENTS PERFE[...] HAVE MADE THEM NOT KOSHER FOR PASSOVER. TO ME THIS WAS THE MOST EXCITING TIME, WATCHING EVERYONE WO[...] THE ROOM. THESE WERE THE LAST MATZOS WE EVER HAD IN MNISZEK.

ALL THROUGH HER LIFE, Passover was Esther's favorite holiday. Although Passover lasts for eight days, for Jewish women it begins long before, as they prepare the house and the special foods that must last through the holiday. Matzo baking was done communally because the oven had to be specially cleaned and purified.

Passover

USE TO BAKE MATZOS. MOTTEL WOULD SCORE THE
THER WOMEN WOULD ROLL OUT. MY MOTHER, WHO IS
HOUT HAVING TO ADD FLOUR OR WATER WHICH WOULD
QUICKLY WITH THE AROMA OF THE MATZOS FILLING
ESTHER NISENTHAL KRINITZ 1998

"March 1939. Every year before Passover, the Jewish women of Mniszek would gather at Mottel the shoemaker's house to bake matzos. Mottel would score the matzos and pass them to his son Yankel to bake. Each woman would make the dough for her own matzos, which the other women would roll out. My mother, who is making the dough here, was one of the best dough makers because she mixed her ingredients perfectly without having to add [more] flour or water, which would have made them not kosher for Passover. To me this was the most exciting time, watching everyone working so quickly with the aroma of the matzos filling the room. These were **the last matzos we ever had in Mniszek.**"

—Esther

The women would take turns making the dough—an exacting and critical task, because it had to be done very quickly. Esther was so proud of her mother because Rachel's matzo dough was always perfect.

While this wasn't the last Passover Esther's family observed, it was the last they celebrated.

SEPTEMBER 1939 MY FRIENDS AND I RAN TO SEE THE FIRST NAZIS ENTERING OUR VILLAGE, MNISZEK THEY STOPPED IN FRONT OF MY
TO ROUGH UP MY GRANDFATHER AND CUT HIS BEARD AS MY GRANDMOTHER SCREAMED
ESTHER NISENTHAL KRINI

HOUSE, WHERE ONE GOT OFF HIS HORSE

Nazis Arrive in Mniszek

"September 1939. My friends and I run to see the first Nazis entering our village, Mniszek. They stopped in front of my grandparents' house, where one got off his horse to rough up my grandfather and cut his beard as my grandmother screamed."

—Esther

ONE DAY, THE WAR ARRIVED. Esther's friends, who lived next door, told her that they had seen hammers and sickles in the moon, a sign that war was coming. After Kristallnacht in November 1938, when German Jews were beaten and murdered in one night of systematic brutality, the Jews of Rachow began to fear for their own fate.

OCTOBER 1939. AS SOON AS THE NAZIS CAME, THEY PUT MOST OF THE MNISZEK BOYS AND GIRLS TO WORK DIGGING TANK TRENCHES ACROSS THE FIELDS, SEEING THAT THE TRENCHES HEADED EAST, MY FATHER PREDICTED THAT THE NAZIS WOULD GO TO WAR AGAINST THE RUSSIANS. NONE OF THESE BOYS AND GIRLS SURVIVED THE WAR.

MECHEL ITZHAK NACHUM
GOLDA ELYA ESTHER NISENTHAL KRINITZ 1996
HERSH RUBEN

Digging Trenches

"October 1939. As soon as the Nazis came, they put most of the Mniszek boys and girls to work digging tank trenches across the fields. Seeing that the trenches headed east, my father predicted that the Nazis would go to war against the Russians. None of these boys and girls survived the war: Itzhak, Mechel, Nachum, Golda, Elya, Hersh, Ruben."

—Esther

AFTER THE GERMAN TROOPS arrived, they made everyone work for them. The women of Mniszek washed their laundry and cooked for them. Esther's mother, Rachel, was ordered to bake for the major in charge of the troops, because she had eggs and could bake beautiful sponge cakes. The young men and the boys and girls old enough to work hard were ordered to dig trenches. Esther was twelve, too young to do heavy labor, but she and ten-year-old Mania would bring food to Ruven and help him with his work.

Although all of my mother's work is a memorial, this one is almost like a roll call, naming each young person who perished.

JULY 1940. I HAD HEARD THAT THE NAZI SOLDIERS HAD A DENTIST IN THEIR CAMP, SO WHEN I DEVELOPED A TERRIBLE TOOTHACHE, I GOT ONE OF MY POLISH FRIENDS TO GO TO THE CAMP WITH ME. SINCE THE GERMANS WOULDN'T HAVE HELPED ME IF THEY HAD KNOWN I WAS JEWISH, I TAUGHT MY FRIEND TO SAY, IN GERMAN, "MY SISTER HAS A TOOTHACHE." AFTER THE DENTIST TOOK OUT MY TOOTH, HE GAVE ME A BAR OF CHOCOLATE. WHEN I GOT HOME, MY MOTHER WAS SHOCKED THAT I HAD HAD THE NERVE TO GO TO THE NAZIS FOR HELP.

ESTHER NISENTHAL KRINITZ 1997

Toothache

"July 1940. I had heard that the Nazi soldiers had a dentist in their camp, so when I developed a terrible toothache, I got one of my Polish friends to go to the camp with me. Since the **Germans wouldn't have helped me if they had known I was Jewish,** I taught my friend to say, in German, 'My sister has a toothache.' After the dentist took out my tooth, he gave me a bar of chocolate. When I got home, my mother was shocked that I had had the nerve to go to the Nazis for help."

—Esther

THE FIRST YEAR or so of German occupation was relatively free of the extreme cruelty that came later. So when my mother developed a terrible toothache, she was not reluctant to turn to the Germans for help. When my mother told this story, she seemed to be as shocked by her daring as her own mother had been.

APRIL 1941, MY MOTHER HAD BROUGHT ME TO WORK FOR A FARMER IN GOŚCIERADOW, NEXT TO THE LA[...]
MANURE, I HEARD SOMEONE CALLING MY NAME. I LOOKED UP TO SEE MY COUSIN MOISHE, I WAS [...]
HOME TO TELL MY MOTHER,

ESTH[...]

Goscieradow

"April 1941. My mother had brought me to work for a farmer in Goscieradow, next to the labor camp. As I was spreading manure, I heard someone calling my name. I looked up to see my cousin Moishe. **I was so sad and wanted to go home** to tell my mother."

—Esther

POOR AS THEY HAD BEEN BEFORE, the war cut off the family's livelihood, and everyone was forced to find work where they could. Esther and Mania each worked for nearby farmers who needed help with farm chores and offered food and a little money in return.

In spring 1941, my mother was working for a farmer in the neighboring village of Goscieradow. She had never been to this farm before, and was shocked to discover that the field where she was spreading manure was next to a labor camp. The men imprisoned here were forced to build roads, split rocks, and other kinds of grueling work. Esther was even more shocked to see her cousin Moishe in the camp, and to hear that his father was there too. Although she worried that he might get into trouble if he were found talking to her, Moishe was anxious to know what had happened to Esther's father and brother.

Esther was always so sad as she described seeing her cousin in such a state.

Erev Pesach

"April 1941. As my father was praying on Erev Pesach, two Nazis showed up and began to beat him. They pulled him outside, ripping off his prayer shawl, and got ready to shoot him. My mother yelled to me and my brother to get the Nazi commander to stop them. The commander wasn't there, but his aide called them off."

—Esther

THE DAY AFTER SHE SAW Moishe, Esther ran home to tell her mother about her cousin. It was Erev Pesach, the day before Passover. Her father, Hersh, was praying, wearing the prayer shawl—*tallis*—and leather phylacteries, called *tefillin*, which Jewish men wrap around their arms and chest. Rachel had set the table with the special Passover dishes, Esther's favorites.

Not long after she got home, two Nazi soldiers walked into their house. Seeing the table set, they tore off the tablecloth, sending all the food and dishes flying. They pulled Hersh out of the house into the yard, tearing off his *tefillin*. Rachel shouted to Esther and Ruven to run to get the Nazi commander. Meanwhile, the commander's aide had heard all the screaming and, stepping out of his nearby quarters, called to the two soldiers to leave Hersh alone.

They obeyed their officer's orders and let Hersh go, but the soldiers weren't finished. They went back into the house and, looking around, discovered the goose under the table, no longer hidden by the cloth. The soldiers grabbed the goose and killed her, which meant that the family would no longer have eggs.

It was a very sad meal. Nothing was left but potatoes. Esther couldn't bring herself to tell her mother about Moishe then—the family had enough troubles of its own.

APRIL 1941. AS MY FATHER WAS PRAYING ON EREV PESACH, TWO NAZIS SHOWED UP AND BEGAN TO BEAT HIM. THEY PULLED HIM OUTSIDE, RIPPING OFF HIS PRAYER SHAWL, AND GOT READY TO SHOOT HIM. MY MOTHER YELLED TO ME AND MY BROTHER TO GET THE NAZI COMMANDER TO STOP THEM. THE COMMANDER WASN'T THERE, BUT HIS AIDE CALLED THEM OFF.

ESTHER Nisental Krinitz 1993

JUNE 1941. MY SISTER AND I BROUGHT OUR COWS TO THE GOOD PASTURE NEAR THE VISTULA RIVER, THROUGH THE TREES, I
PRISON CAMP, WHICH THE NAZIS HAD TURNED INTO A DEATH CAMP FOR THE JEWISH BOYS, AFTER THEY WERE BEATEN UNTIL T
WERE LED INTO THE BIRCH FOREST AND SHOT.

WE WERE NEXT TO THE JANISZEW
O LONGER WORK ON THE DAM, THEY
EN THAL KRINITZ 1994

Janiszow
(heaven and hell)

"June 1941. My sister and I brought our cows to the good pasture near the Vistula River. Through the trees, I discovered we were next to the Janiszow prison camp, which the Nazis had turned into **a death camp for the Jewish boys.** After they were beaten until they could no longer work on the dam, they were led into the birch forest and shot."

—Esther

THE LOSS OF THE FAMILY'S GOOSE was very hard because by this point, Jews were no longer allowed to own any livestock. Esther's family still had one forbidden cow, which they hid with neighbors.

Esther and Mania were looking after the cows of the Polish farmer whom Mania was working for. The best pasture was near the Vistula River, so Esther and Mania decided to take the cows there on a particularly beautiful June day.

As the cows wandered closer to the river, Esther could tell that they were next to the Janiszow prison camp. Through the trees, Esther saw Jewish prisoners, wearing Star of David armbands. Mania quickly left with her cows, but Esther held on to her cow and stayed. She watched as a young man was led into the woods; shortly after, Esther heard a shot. Then she took her cow and headed back.

JULY 1942. MY FATHER HAD BEEN COLLECTING PINE TAR FOR A LOCAL LANDOWNER WHEN THE GESTAPO ORDERED MY
BROTHER RUBEN TO REPORT TO JANISZEW LABOR CAMP. MY MOTHER PLEADED WITH MY FATHER TO GO IN MY BROTHER'S PLACE, CRYING
THAT HE WOULD NOT SURVIVE AFTER HIS RECENT RECOVERY FROM TYPHOID. MY FATHER SAID THAT NEITHER ONE OF THEM WOULD GO,
AND TOOK MY BROTHER INTO THE FOREST WITH HIM. THEY HAD BUILT A HUT FOR THEMSELVES, WHERE THEY SLEPT AND WORKED.
FOR THE REST OF THAT SUMMER, MY MOTHER WOULD BRING FOOD TO THEM, AND SOMETIMES I WOULD GO WITH HER.

ESTHER NISENTHAL KRINITZ 1996

The Pine Forest

"July 1942. My father had been collecting pine tar for a local landowner when the Gestapo ordered my brother Ruven to report to Janiszow labor camp. My mother pleaded with my father to go in my brother's place, crying that he would not survive after his recent recovery from typhoid. My father said that neither one of them would go, and took my brother into the forest with him. They had built a hut for themselves, where they slept and worked. For the rest of that summer, my mother would bring food to them, and sometimes I would go with her."

—Esther

AFTER SEEING FIRSTHAND what the Janiszow camp was like, Esther and her family were horrified when Ruven was ordered to report there. But at this point, in July 1942, Rachel and Hersh were still fighting back. Rachel just wanted to save her son, already weakened from typhus, and she was even willing to ask her husband to sacrifice himself in his son's place. But Hersh decided that instead, he and Ruven would live in the forest, tapping pine tar to sell to the farmers for turpentine.

Dawn Raid

"September 1942. This was a prelude to the Final Solution that followed. At dawn, the Gestapo made a surprise raid and in our nightshirts, lined us up by the river and terrorized us with their guns as our Polish neighbors looked on."

—Esther

BY SEPTEMBER, the weather was turning colder and Hersh and Ruven returned home. Mania was still working for and living with a farmer in a neighboring town.

One morning, before dawn, Nazi soldiers began banging on their door, screaming at the family to get out of their house. They marched Esther and her family across the road, still in their nightclothes, and lined them up along the riverbank, raising their guns and preparing to shoot.

As the neighbors stood by and watched, one ran off to get the sheriff and to warn the other Jews in the village. When the sheriff arrived, he tried to persuade the soldiers to let the family go home. "We know these people! They've lived here all their lives!" he said.

Dawn Raid II

"September 1942. I went back to the house to get clothes for my family when a soldier appeared and struck me with his rifle for not raising my hands quickly."
—Esther

SEPTEMBER 1942 I WENT BACK TO THE HOUSE TO GET CLOTHES FOR MY FAMILY WHEN A SOLDIER APPEARED AND STRUCK ME WITH HIS RIFLE FOR NOT RAISING MY HANDS QUICKLY
ESTHER NISENTHAL KRINITZ 1992

RACHEL PLEADED WITH THE SOLDIERS to let Esther go in the house and bring them some clothes. Esther was so confused and in shock that all she could manage to pull out of the wardrobe were socks, draped across her arm in the picture. The soldier who had followed Esther into the house grew angry with her for taking too long, and struck her in the face with his gun. Esther ran back outside then, with an armful of socks and a bloody mouth.

SEPTEMBER 1942   AFTER THE MORNING RAID THE GESTAPO WERE RETURNING WE FLED
ACROSS THE FIELDS TO THE WOODS, MY MOTHER DIRECTING ME TO SEPARATE.
                                    ESTHER NISENTHAL KRINITZ 1992.

Fleeing Across the Fields

"September 1942. After the morning raid, the Gestapo were returning. We fled across the fields to the woods, my mother directing me to separate."

—Esther

WHEN THE FAMILY RETURNED home, they found their neighbors had ransacked their house. As Rachel fixed the family a meager breakfast, Ruven ran into the house, shouting that the soldiers were returning. Hersh and Ruven headed to the river to hide in the marsh grass. Rachel and Esther and the two little girls fled in the opposite direction, up the hill from the house and into the woods. Rachel's instincts were to scatter, and she directed Esther to go off on her own, to the right, while she and Chana and Leah went to the left.

Esther fled into the woods, and soon after, met her cousin Golda, also in hiding. Golda was near crazed with fear over what would befall her elderly parents, who had been left at home. Esther and Golda stayed in the woods for hours, Golda sobbing all the while. Finally, when they saw the soldiers leaving, they headed for home. As they emerged from the woods, they saw Hersh coming toward them, and Golda could tell from his face that something terrible had happened to her parents. She fell to the ground in a faint. What she had feared was true: the Gestapo had come to their house and killed the old couple.

Saying Good-bye

"This was my family on the morning of October 15, 1942. We were ordered by the Gestapo to leave our homes by 10 A.M. to join all the other Jews on the road to Krasnik railroad station and then to their deaths."
—Esther

THE NIGHT BEFORE her family had to leave their home, Esther was frantic, determined not to go to Krasnik. She begged her parents to think of someone who was not Jewish who might take her in. Her parents were reluctant at first, but then Rachel turned to Hersh and said, "Maybe Stefan."

That was all Esther needed—a name. Not wanting to go alone, she decided that Mania would go with her to the home of their father's friend. Rachel kissed her eldest daughters, and sent them off. "Good-bye, my children," she said. "Maybe you will live."

THIS WAS MY FAMILY ON THE MORNING OF OCTOBER 15, 1942. WE WERE ORDERED BY THE GESTAPO TO LEAVE OUR HOMES BY 10 A.M. TO JOIN ALL THE OTHER JEWS ON THE ROAD TO KRASNIK RAILROAD STATION AND THEN TO THEIR DEATH.

ESTHER KRINITZ 1991

Leaving for Good

"October 15, 1942. We left our house for good and walked down to the road. Mottel sat in the front wagon holding the Torah. My parents went to join him while my brother helped my little sisters settle into the rear wagon with my aunt Trushel, her sister Golda, my uncle Ruven, and my five little cousins. Suddenly Mottel's daughter-in-law stood up and cried to my mother, 'Rachel, we will never come back! We will all perish!' Everyone began to cry. Mania and I followed quickly behind the woman who was to take us to Dombrowa and the house of Stefan, my father's friend. The wagons left for the Krasnik station, and we never saw our family again."

—Esther

OCTOBER 15, 1942. WE LEFT OUR HOUSE FOR GOOD AND WALKED DOWN TO THE ROAD. MOTTEL SAT IN THE FRONT WAGON HOLDING THE TORAH. MY PARENTS WENT TO JOIN HIM WHILE MY BROTHER HELPED MY LITTLE SISTERS SETTLE INTO THE REAR WAGON WITH MY AUNT TRUSHEL, HER SISTER GOLDA, MY UNCLE RUVEN, AND MY FIVE LITTLE COUSINS. SUDDENLY MOTTEL'S DAUGHTER-IN-LAW STOOD UP AND CRIED TO MY MOTHER, "RACHEL, WE WILL NEVER COME BACK! WE WILL ALL PERISH!" EVERYONE BEGAN TO CRY. MANIA AND I FOLLOWED QUICKLY BEHIND THE WOMAN WHO WAS TO TAKE US TO DOMBROWA AND THE HOUSE OF STEFAN, MY FATHER'S FRIEND. THE WAGONS LEFT FOR THE KRASNIK STATION, AND WE NEVER SAW OUR FAMILY AGAIN.   ESTHER NISENTHAL KRINITZ   JUNE 1998

ON FRIDAY OCTOBER.15 1942 IT WAS THE BEGINNING OF THE END THE SOMBER MARCH OF THE RACHOW JEWS TO THEIR DEATHS
ESTHER NISENTAL KRINITZ 1991.

The Jews of Rachow

"On Friday, October 15, 1942, it was the beginning of the end, the somber march of the Rachow Jews to their deaths."

—Esther

THE GERMANS had ordered all the Jews in the Rachow district to leave their homes and report to the train station in Krasnik. Anyone who failed to do so would be shot. The Jews were directed to take only their money and their jewelry.

No one knew for sure where they were going. Esther's mother told her they might be going to a ghetto. But Esther believed that death would be waiting for them wherever they were taken.

When their mother agreed to let Esther and Mania go to Stefan's house, she paid a neighbor to take them there. But instead, the woman took them to her brother's house and left. Once they realized that they had been abandoned, the girls fled, knowing that there was a bounty for Jews. They came to the Krasnik road, and there saw all the Jews of Rachow piled into their wagons on the way to the train station. It was a devastating sight. Everyone was crying; some of them, wrapped in their prayer shawls, cried to God.

OCTOBER 15, 1942 AFTER BEING ABANDONED BY A NEIGHBOR WHOM MY MOTHER HAD PAID TO TAKE US TO DOMBROWA, MANIA AND I MET OUR
COUSIN DINA, ON HER WAY TO KRASNIK WITH HER BABY AND THE OTHER RACHOV JEWS, AS THE ROAD BEGAN TO CURVE AROUND THE MOUNTAIN,
I REALIZED HOW CLOSE WE WERE TO KRASNIK, AND I WAS SUDDENLY TERRIFIED, I PLEADED WITH MANIA TO COME WITH ME TO
STEFAN, SHE FINALLY AGREED AFTER DINA TOLD HER, "GO MANIA, GO WITH ESTHER".   ESTHER NISENTHAL KRINITZ 1994

Dina

"October 15, 1942. After being abandoned by a neighbor whom my mother had paid to take us to Dombrowa, Mania and I met our cousin Dina, on her way to Krasnik with her baby and the other Rachow Jews. As the road began to curve around the mountain, I realized how close we were to Krasnik and I was suddenly terrified. I pleaded with Mania to come with me to Stefan. She finally agreed after Dina told her, 'Go, Mania, go with Esther.'"

—Esther

WHEN MANIA AND ESTHER SAW their cousin Dina with her baby on the Krasnik road, Mania ran and clung to her, relieved to be reunited with a member of her family. They continued along the road together for some time. But once Esther saw the curve in the road ahead, she had a terrible premonition of death and realized that she couldn't go on. She turned to Mania and insisted that they try to find their way to Stefan's. Mania refused. It wasn't until Dina intervened and told her to go with Esther that Mania finally relented.

OCTOBER IS 1942. MY SISTER AND I ARRIVED IN THE VILLAGE OF DOMBROWA AND WENT TO THE HOUSE OF STEFAN OUR FATH... PROMISED TO HELP, BUT AFTER TWO DAYS, HE SENT US OUT INTO THE RAIN, WITH NO PLACE TO GO BUT THE FOREST.

WE BEGGED HIM TO HELP US. HE EMBRACED US AND
...NTHAL KRINITZ 1992

Stefan's House

"October 15, 1942. My sister and I arrived in the village of Dombrowa and went to the house of Stefan, our father's friend. We begged him to help us. He embraced us and promised to help. But after two days, he sent us out into the rain, with no place to go but the forest."

—Esther

STEFAN HID ESTHER AND MANIA in his attic, but on their third day there he said, "You must go. All Mniszek knows you are here. The Nazis will come, they'll kill you, they'll kill my family, and they'll burn my farm."

Esther realized that it was just a matter of time before the Gestapo would come searching for them. They would have to go where no one knew them, and where they could pass as Polish Catholics. So Esther created new identities for them: Esther would become Josephine, or Juszia, in Polish; Mania would become Maria, or Marisha. They would say they came from Czyzow, a village that Esther had heard her father talk about. Esther made Mania promise that she would sear these new identities into her mind and never speak Yiddish again.

OCTOBER 24 1942 I CAME OUT OF THE THICK WOODS, ON THE ROAD FROM KSIEŻOMIERZ AND WAS TERRIFIED. I FOUND MYS
GERMAN, WHERE I WAS GOING, I KEPT SAYING, IN POLISH, I DONT UNDERSTAND FINALLY A POLISH-SPEAKING GUAR
THE OFFICER LAUGHED AND WAVED ME ON. ESTHER NISENTHAL KRINITZ 1993

ESTHER AND MANIA made their way to the village of Ksiezomierz. They found work, but after several days the families that hired them asked for identification papers. Esther pretended to take the ferry to Czyzow to get them, but instead made her way to Mniszek, to find out what had become of her family.

Along the way, Esther came upon German barracks. A soldier stepped forward into the road and said, in German, "Halt!" Esther acted as though she couldn't understand. Then another soldier appeared, and in Polish, said, "Where are you going, little girl?"

ONT OF GESTAPO BARRACKS, AN OFFICER ASKED ME, IN
ASK ME, AND I SAID I WAS GOING TO MY GRANDMOTHER'S

Ksiezomierz

"October 24, 1942. I came out of the thick woods on the road from Ksiezomierz and was terrified. I found myself in front of Gestapo barracks. An officer asked me, in German, where I was going. I kept saying, in Polish, I don't understand. Finally, a Polish-speaking guard came to ask me, and I said I was going to my grandmother's. The officer laughed and waved me on."

—Esther

"I'm going to my grandmother's," Esther said, thinking of Little Red Riding Hood. They let her pass. When she got to Mniszek, she went to her neighbor Zebina's house. Zebina told her that when the Jews arrived in Krasnik, the Germans shot at them randomly and covered the square with bodies. Esther returned to Ksiezomierz the next day and told the families that the ferry to Czyzow wasn't running and she hadn't been able to get their papers. She didn't tell Mania what she had heard from Zebina.

OCTOBER 30 1942, MANIA AND I LEFT THE VILLAGE OF KSIEZOMIESZ
AFTER WE WERE ASKED TO GET BIRTH CERTIFICATES FROM THE PLACE WE
SAID WE CAME FROM. INSTEAD WE WENT TO THE DEPTHS OF THE FOREST
AND WAITED FOR NIGHT FALL.   ESTHER NISENTHAL KRINITZ 1994

Depths of the Forest

"October 30, 1942. Mania and I left the village of Ksiezomierz after we were asked to get birth certificates from the place we said we came from. Instead we went to the depths of the forest and waited for nightfall."

—Esther

THE FAMILIES ESTHER AND MANIA worked for were insistent about papers. Esther said she would try again to go to Czyzow, but this time, she took Mania with her, knowing they would not return. To avoid going past the military barracks again, the girls went through the thick forest, where few people went because of the wild pigs that were known to live there. They armed themselves with sticks, and waited in the forest until dark.

OCTOBER 30 1942. AFTER DARK WE WENT TO THE HOUSE OF OUR FORMER NEIGHBOR ŻEBINA. AS HER DAUGHTERS, OUR FRIENDS, WATCHED, SHE TOLD US WE
HAD TO LEAVE BECAUSE THE GESTAPO WERE LOOKING FOR JEWS IN THE DARKEST NIGHT WE HEADED FOR THE WOODS BUT STUMBLED
INTO A PILE OF DEBRIS WHERE WE SPENT THE NIGHT.   ESTHER NISENTHAL KRINITZ 1994

Zebina

"October 30, 1942. After dark we went to the house of our former neighbor Zebina. As her daughters, our friends, watched, she told us we had to leave because the Gestapo were looking for Jews. In the darkest night, we headed for the woods but stumbled into a pile of debris where we spent the night."

—Esther

THIS TIME WHEN THEY ARRIVED at her house, Zebina was terrified to see Esther and Mania, cursing them and ordering them to go away and never return. Her daughters silently watched in the window. Esther and Mania felt their way through the fields and finally stumbled into a pile of debris where they slept for the night.

Mania and Esther ran to Zalesia, about a kilometer away, and then on to another village nearby called Grabowka. Esther decided they would go to the sheriff's house and ask him for help. "If we're found hiding in the forest," she said, "people will know we're Jewish. And if we're going to be Juszia and Marisha, we have to act as they would." After hearing Esther's story, the sheriff said that Mania could stay with him and his mother. He placed Esther with an old farmer whose wife was sickly and bedridden, and needed someone to help him look after the animals and keep house.

The Sky Is Falling

"In early November 1942, Mania and I made our way to the village of Grabowka, where we told people that we were Polish Catholic farm girls who had been separated from our family after our farm was taken over by Folksdeutsche. The night after we arrived, I had a dream that my mother came to get me, running and pulling me along. 'Why are we running?' I asked her. She said, 'Because the black sky is falling, and when it reaches the ground, we will die.' When I looked back, black pieces of clouds were falling to the earth."

—Esther

ESTHER WOKE UP from her dream to find the farmer shaking her, telling her that she had to hide in the barn. The Germans were in the village and were rounding up young boys and girls to take them off to Germany as slave laborers. Esther hid under piles of straw in the attic of the barn until the Germans left. Later, she came to believe that her dream had been a warning of danger.

JANUARY 1943 ONE DAY IN GRABOWKA, WHILE WORKING FOR THE OLD COUPLE, WHO TOOK ME IN, I WENT TO THE WELL AND WAS SURPRISED TO SEE IT SURROUNDED BY GESTAPO OFFICERS. I STARTED TO DRAW THE WATER WHEN ONE CAME OVER, AND SPEAKING POLISH, OFFERED TO HELP. I THANKED HIM AND HE CLICKED HIS HEELS IN RESPONSE.

ESTHER NISENTHAL KRINITZ 1994.

The Well

"January 1943. One day in Grabowka, while working for the old couple who took me in, I went to the well and was surprised to see it surrounded by Gestapo officers. I started to draw the water when one came over and, speaking Polish, offered to help. I thanked him and he clicked his heels in response."

—Esther

EVERY DAY, my mother would go to the village well for water. Drawing water was not an easy job, but there were always people around to help. On this day, though, only German soldiers were in the vicinity, so my mother struggled to turn the wheel on her own. Much to her surprise, one soldier offered to help, and when he was done, she found herself thanking him. She wondered how he would have felt had he known she was Jewish.

JUNE 1943, IN GRABOWKA. WHILE I WAS TENDING THE GARDEN I HAD PLANTED, TWO NAZI SOLDIERS APPEARED AND BEGAN TO TALK TO ME. I COULDN'T LET THEM KNOW THAT I COULD UNDERSTAND THEM, SO I JUST SHOOK MY HEAD AS THEY SPOKE. DZIADEK, THE OLD FARMER WHO HAD TAKEN ME IN AS HIS HOUSEKEEPER, CAME TO STAND WATCH NEARBY, BUT THE HONEY BEES RESCUED ME FIRST, SUDDENLY SWARMING AROUND THE SOLDIERS. "WHY AREN'T THEY STINGING YOU, ?" THE SOLDIERE ASKED DZIADEK AS THEY RAN OUT OF THE GARDEN.

ESTHER NISENTAL KRINITZ 1996

The Bees

"June 1943, in Grabowka. While I was tending the garden I had planted, two Nazi soldiers appeared and began to talk to me. I couldn't let them know that I understood them, so I just shook my head as they spoke. Dziadek, the old farmer who had taken me in as his housekeeper, came to stand watch nearby, but **the honeybees rescued me** first, swarming around the soldiers. 'Why aren't they stinging you?' the soldier asked Dziadek as they ran out of the garden."

—Esther

THE OLD FARMER GREW to depend on Esther, his young and energetic housekeeper. She came to call him Dziadek—Grandfather. Esther loved Dziadek's gift for growing. He had a beautiful orchard, with apple, pear, cherry, and plum trees, and he and Esther planted a big garden each year. One June day, while Esther was weeding in the strawberry beds, two Nazi soldiers entered the garden. Esther knew from the way they cruelly trampled her plants that they brought danger. Dziadek stood by to watch out for her, but in this instance, even Dziadek could not help her. But the bees could sense the strangers among them—from their scents, my mother believed—and they came and drove off the soldiers. "The bees saved me!" my mother would say with a laugh.

Zayde

"A year later, in Grabowka, I dreamed that I went to see my grandfather in his house. My grandfather had died three years earlier, and in my dream, I knew that I had to keep my distance from him. 'Oh, Zayde,' I cried, 'you are close to God! You have to help me!'

'Don't worry, Esther,' he said. 'You will cross the river and you will be safe.'"

—Esther

DESPITE THE KINDNESS of those who took them in, Esther felt desperate and worried all the time in Grabowka, always expecting someone to find them out and take them away. During this fear-filled time, Esther dreamed of her grandfather, a very devout man whom she believed was especially close to God. In her dream, she stood before her grandfather in his house, crying and pleading for him to help her. Her grandfather told her not to worry, and reassured her that she would be safe. This dream was meaningful to Esther not only because it helped to calm her fears but also because it was the only time she could allow herself to cry.

JULY 1944 AT SUNDOWN, RUSSIAN INFANTRY MARCHED INTO THE VILLAGE GRABOWKA, THE NEIGHBORS AND I, RUSHED TO THE FENCE TO LOOK AT THE SOLDIERS. WE OFFERED THEM WATER, WHICH THEY WERE DESPERATE FOR, BUT THEIR SERGEANT ORDERED THEM TO KEEP MARCHING. FINALLY FREEDOM HAD COME FOR MANIA AND ME, BUT FOR THE REST OF OUR FAMILY IT WAS TOO LATE.   ESTHER NISENTHAL KRINITZ 1995

Freedom

"July 1944. At sundown, Russian infantry marched into the village of Grabowka. The neighbors and I rushed to the fence to look at the soldiers. We offered them water, which they were desperate for, but their sergeant ordered them to keep marching. Finally, freedom had come for Mania and me, but for the rest of our family, it was too late."

—Esther

BY 1944, PEOPLE IN GRABOWKA were beginning to hear rumors that the Germans were losing the war. Then one day, a small patrol of about twenty-five soldiers marched into the village. When Esther heard their leader's call to them in Russian, her heart soared. The war was over. She wanted to pinch herself—she was free! She and Mania were free!

AUGUST 1944. AFTER THE LIBERATION, I LEFT GRABOWKA AND RETURNED TO MNISZEK. NONE OF MY FAMILY WAS THERE. I WENT TO MAIDANEK TO SEARCH FOR SIGNS OF THEM. I LOOKED THROUGH THE PILES OF WORN SHOES BUT THEY ALL LOOKED THE SAME. AFTER SEEING THE SHOWERS AND GAS CHAMBERS, THE CREMATORIUM, AND THE GIANT CABBAGES GROWING ON HUMAN ASHES, I JOINED THE POLISH AND RUSSIAN ARMIES STATIONED THERE.

ESTHER NISENTHAL KRINITZ
OCTOBER 1995

Maidanek

"August 1944. After the liberation, I left Grabowka and returned to Mniszek. None of my family was there. I went to Maidanek to search for signs of them. I looked through the piles of worn shoes but they all looked the same. After seeing the showers and gas chambers, the crematorium, and the giant cabbages growing on human ashes, I joined the Polish and Russian armies stationed there."

—Esther

ESTHER'S FIRST IMPULSE was to rush back to Mniszek to find out if any of her family had survived. None of them had returned. But neighbors said that Esther might find signs of her family at Maidanek, a concentration camp outside of Lublin.

In this picture, Esther arrives at the gates to Maidanek. After the Russians liberated the camp, they made it the headquarters for the combined Russian and Polish armies. Esther began to comb through piles of shoes, but there were thousands and thousands, all dust-covered, worn, and indistinguishable from one another.

Esther tried to capture in this image all that she saw and would later learn about Maidanek. She placed rows of giant cabbages growing on a field made rich by human ashes. She narrated the killing that took place in the adjacent Krepicki Forest, where 18,000 Jews were slaughtered in one day in November 1943. She also included metal canisters, which the Germans filled with ashes and sold to Polish families who believed they were reclaiming the remains of their loved ones who had been taken to the camp at Buchenwald.

Horrified by what she saw at Maidanek, but inspired by the courage and determination of the Russians, Esther joined the Polish Army.

MARCH 1945 ALONG WITH THE 5TH DIVISION OF THE RUSSIAN ARMY, MY POLISH ARMY UNIT CROSSED THE ODER RIVER INTO GERMANY. WE PASSED
HAD HUNG NAZI OFFICERS ON EVERY TREE ALONG THE ROAD. THEY LOOKED AS THOUGH THEY WERE STILL ALIVE. MANY OTHER DEAD NAZIS LAY
WHICH A YOUNG PRETTY RUSSIAN SOLDIER STOOD, POINTING THE WAY TO BERLIN.

EST

OF AN EARLIER BATTLE. THE RUSSIANS
ACROSS THE FIELD, AT THE EDGE OF
IAL Krinitz 1998

To Germany

"March 1945. Along with the 5th Division of the Russian Army, my Polish Army unit crossed the Oder River into Germany. We passed the site of an earlier battle. **The Russians had hung Nazi officers on every tree along the road.** They looked as though they were still alive. Many other dead Nazis lay scattered along across the field, at the edge of which a young pretty Russian soldier stood, pointing the way to Berlin."

—Esther

COMING TO AMERICA, JUNE 10 1949 WE ARRIVED IN NEW YORK. MAX'S COUSIN CLARA CAME ABOARD THE SHIP TO GREET US. AS OUR DAUGHTER BRASIA SLEPT IN HER FATHER'S ARMS, CLARA SAID TO HER, "MY DEAR CHILD, THIS WILL BE YOUR AMERICA!"

ESTHER NISENTHAL KRINITZ 1996

Coming to America

"Coming to America, June 10, 1949. We arrived in New York. Max's cousin Clara came aboard the ship to greet us. As our daughter Brasia slept in her father's arms, Clara said to her, 'My dear child, this will be your America!'"

—Esther

ONCE THE WAR ENDED, Esther and Mania went to a refugee camp in Germany, one of many Displaced Persons, or DP, camps set up by the Allies. Before they left the camp, they had each married. Max Krinitz had relatives in New York, so Max and Esther applied to emigrate to the United States. Mania and her husband, Lipa, went to Israel.

Max and Esther had to wait for their immigration papers, though, and while they were waiting, my mother became pregnant. Not wanting his child to be born in a DP camp, my father went to Belgium, where he could find work. He soon sent for my mother, and I was born in Belgium in 1947.

Finally, our immigration papers came through. We sailed for New York in June 1949. Esther was so excited when the ship entered New York Harbor and she saw the Statue of Liberty. For Esther, coming to America meant that she would never again be persecuted for being Jewish.

At her very essence, our mother was a gifted storyteller. Esther's drive to tell her story of survival ultimately found its best expression in her needle and thread. She understood that the world must not forget the Holocaust, recognized the power of her pictures to carry her message, and knew that these would be her legacy.

I remember the point, as a young child, when I was struck by the realization that Mommy had been a fugitive, in hiding for her survival. I was so proud of her courage and cunning, I was eager to tell my friends. I think that this, in turn, made her proud—knowing that her daughters had become tellers of her story.

These pages fulfill our mother's dream to see her pictures and story in a book. May these images and words keep her memories close, and may they inspire us all to keep telling the story.

—Helene McQuade

APPRECIATIONS

In their own way, many people have helped to bring Esther's story to light, and we would like to extend to a number of them our heartfelt thanks: Ronni Denes, Doris Freedman, Lisa Hill, Benita Kline, and Nina Shapiro Perl of Art and Remembrance; Anita Semjen of the Cultural Exchange Foundation; Meg and Larry Kasdan, Bill and Marcie Cohen Ferris, Ruth and Joe Bell, Rebecca Hoffberger and Mark Ward of the American Visionary Art Museum; Louise Weiner, Tom Freudenheim, Larry Shire, Karen Gottlieb, Liza Baker, and David Winter.

Because they were always foremost in Esther's mind, we dedicate this book to Esther's family: her grandchildren Rachel, Simon, and John Henry; her sister Mania and her children, Harry and Rachel and their families; her sons-in-law, Bruce and Jack; and to the memories of those whose deaths preceded Esther's, including her husband and our father, Max Krinitz.

—Bernice Steinhardt and Helene McQuade